Little RIDDLERS

Dorset & Somerset Poets

Edited By Machaela Gavaghan

First published in Great Britain in 2018 by:

Young Writers
Remus House
Coltsfoot Drive
Peterborough
PE2 9BF
Telephone: 01733 890066
Website: www.youngwriters.co.uk

Book Design by Ashley Janson

SB ISBN 978-1-78896-878-2
Printed and bound in the UK by BookPrintingUK
Website: www.bookprintinguk.com
YB0378XZ

FOREWORD

Dear Reader,

Are you ready to get your thinking caps on to puzzle your way through this wonderful collection?

Young Writers' Little Riddlers competition set out to encourage young writers to create their own riddles. Their answers could be whatever or whoever their imaginations desired; from people to places, animals to objects, food to seasons. Riddles are a great way to further the children's use of poetic expression, including onomatopoeia and similes, as well as encourage them to 'think outside the box' by providing clues without giving the answer away immediately.

All of us here at Young Writers believe in the importance of inspiring young children to produce creative writing, including poetry, and we feel that seeing their own riddles in print will keep that creative spirit burning brightly and proudly.

We hope you enjoy riddling your way through this book as much as we enjoyed reading all the entries.

CONTENTS

Manorside Combined School, Parkstone

St Walburga's Catholic Primary School, Moordown

Harry Samuel Jose (6) 142
Catalina Mya Arbelaez Correa (6) 143
Freya Murray (6) 144
Ellie Grace Samath Nicholson (6) 145
Cianán McCaffrey (5) 146
Katie Fendley (6) 147
Lulu Jenkins (5) 148
Maria Pickering (6) 149
Ellie Parry (6) 150
Adam Bujak (6) 151
Eden Grant (6) 152
Oliver Lloyd (6) 153
Stanley Bagnall (6) 154
Erin Barber-Miller (6) 155
Jaden Legaspi-Harvey (6) 156
Autumn Hume (6) 157
Sofia Jakubowska (6) 158
Noah Abonyi (6) 159
Freya Comman (5) 160
Maja Boroszko (6) 161
Zofia Tomczyk (6) 162
Violet Wasmuth (6) 163
Juliette Pegrum (6) 164
Dixie Garton (5) 165
Elizabeth Stalley (6) 166
Sunday Assey (5) 167
Ziyana-Jean Clark (6) 168

Sunninghill Preparatory School, South Walks

Kitty Taschner (7) 169
Iris Høyvåg (6) 170
William Hall (7) 171
Gregory A Vaisyan (7) 172
Charlie Flower (7) 173
Anna Wright (6) 174
Samuel Laurence Roger Lawn (7) 175
Clara Telfer (7) 176
Rex Woollam (7) 177

THE POEMS

Yum

I can be big
I can be small
I can be round like a ball
Some children eat me for their snacks
I come in bags
I come in packs
You can buy me at the shops
I ruin your teeth but I don't care
I come in flavours -
Strawberry, Coke, raspberry and pear
What am I?

Answer: Sweets.

Genny Jones (6)
Heatherlands Primary School, Parkstone

Fashion

We are twins.
We are stylish.
We are changeable.
We sometimes have long legs.
We sometimes have short legs.
We sometimes have no legs.
We come in different sizes and colours.
We are with you everywhere you go.
What are we?

Answer: Shoes.

Cairo Shaw (6)
Heatherlands Primary School, Parkstone

Treetops

I have really long arms and only two legs
and a curly-wurly tail.
These help me swing high in the treetops.
I eat lots of fruit and play with my friends.
Oo, oo, ah, ah!
I live in tropical forests.
What am I?

Answer: A spider monkey.

Bethany Small (6)
Heatherlands Primary School, Parkstone

Beep, Beep

I am very long.
I can be very tall.
You might see me yellow or blue.
I can carry lots of people, even you!
I have four wheels.
I have lots of windows.
To ride on me, you will need a ticket.
What am I?

Answer: A bus.

Ellenah Mae Beney (5)

Heatherlands Primary School, Parkstone

The Sunny Place

Children walking in the sand,
Drawing pictures with their hands.
I got water up my nose,
I have seaweed between my toes.
Making castles, finding shells,
I love the summer in the waves.
What is it?

Answer: A beach.

Kiara Zara Tresova (6)
Heatherlands Primary School, Parkstone

What Am I?

I am small and I am hard
I live in the yard
I eat all the grass
But I'm not very fast
I have four legs and a very small head
And if I get scared, I'll hide in my pen
What am I?

Answer: A tortoise.

Keira-Mae Dunnings (6)
Heatherlands Primary School, Parkstone

Bounce Power

I live in Australia
I am quite large
I have a big tail and big, bouncy, black legs
I bounce around the outback
My baby is called a joey
I keep my baby in a pouch
What am I?

Answer: A kangaroo.

Phillipa May Grady (6)
Heatherlands Primary School, Parkstone

A Food

I am very nice.
I begin with the word 'ice'.
You can get me in piles of different flavours.
Sometimes I'm in a pot.
Sometimes I'm in a cone.
What am I?

Answer: An ice cream.

Jayke Frampton (6)
Heatherlands Primary School, Parkstone

Pretty Pollen

I live in the ground.
I try to reach the sky.
I need sun and water to grow.
I come in lots of colours and I smell really nice.
Bees like to visit me.
What am I?

Answer: A flower.

Chloe Millard (6)
Heatherlands Primary School, Parkstone

Lilly

I sleep anywhere
Any table, any chair
Open drawer, empty shoe
Anybody's lap will do
I know how to miaow
But I don't know how to bark
What am I?

Answer: A cat.

Maja Filipiak (6)
Heatherlands Primary School, Parkstone

Winter Fun

I have a carrot for my nose.
I am cold.
I have black button eyes.
I am made in winter.
Children love to make me.
I melt in the sun.
What am I?

Answer: A snowman.

Alexandra Ava Wallace (6)
Heatherlands Primary School, Parkstone

Fluttery Insect

I start life as a caterpillar.
I come out of a cocoon.
I have wings.
I have antennae.
I can fly.
My wings are lots of colours.
What am I?

Answer: A butterfly.

Sophie Jefferis (6)
Heatherlands Primary School, Parkstone

My Pet

I have a wet nose
I have paws, not toes
I like to run all day
I like to bark and play
My fur has spots
I love my ball lots
Who am I?

Answer: Alfie (my dog).

Mia Ellen Rose Smith (6)
Heatherlands Primary School, Parkstone

Best Friend

My best friend is Oscar.
I don't like dogs.
I have a long tail.
I love to sleep.
I have four legs.
I miaow a lot.
What am I?

Answer: A cat (Chubbs).

Oscar Davies (6)
Heatherlands Primary School, Parkstone

My Friend

Floppy ears each side of my head
Fast paws under me
A wet nose at the front
A wagging tail on the end
In-between is my best friend
What am I?

Answer: A dog.

Sofia Dudek (6)
Heatherlands Primary School, Parkstone

My Soft Friend

I have two sticky-up ears.
I am soft and fluffy.
I am cuddly.
I like to jump and hop.
I like to eat carrots.
I am a pet.
What am I?

Answer: A rabbit.

Naomi Ella Weston (6)
Heatherlands Primary School, Parkstone

Best Friend

I am fluffy.
I have four legs.
I like to live with people.
I like to go on walks.
I play a lot.
I like balls.
What am I?

Answer: A dog.

Finley Cooper Jacomb (6)
Heatherlands Primary School, Parkstone

Strong

I start as a calf.
I have four legs.
I have twelve toes and a big nose.
I am the same colour.
I have short legs.
What am I?

Answer: A rhino.

Henry White (6)
Heatherlands Primary School, Parkstone

Shiny Toy

It makes funny noises.
It is squeaky.
It has a string on the bottom.
It is very, very fun.
It is very shiny.
What is it?

Answer: A balloon.

Nusrat Jahan (6)
Heatherlands Primary School, Parkstone

Fluffiest Thing

I am a fluffy pet.
I have four legs and I like to run.
I have big ears and I make big noises.
What am I?

Answer: A chinchilla.

Smilte Stefanija Sudikaite (6)
Heatherlands Primary School, Parkstone

Woof, Woof

I can be small.
I can be big.
I eat bones.
I live in a kennel.
I like to go for a walk.
What am I?

Answer: A dog.

Joshua Hugh Tomalin (6)
Heatherlands Primary School, Parkstone

The Mystery Vegetable

I am orange and green at the top.
I grow in a field and you can pick me out of the dirty soil.
I am crunchy and tasty when you eat me.
I don't have any seeds in me.
I am very, very hard.
I am the hardest vegetable in the world.
What am I?

Answer: A carrot.

Isaac Richards (6)
Hindhayes Infant School, Street

Fun Ride

I have wheels but I can have two or three.
You can ride me any day.
I sometimes have patterns on me.
I am made from metal.
I look like a capital 'L'.
You push me with your foot whenever you ride me.
What am I?

Answer: A scooter.

Oscar Dutson (6)
Hindhayes Infant School, Street

A Fluffy Toy

You can buy me in a shop.
I can be lots of different colours.
I can make you smile and laugh.
I also have a very dark black nose.
I am soft and cuddly to snuggle.
I can help you get to sleep at night.
What am I?

Answer: A teddy bear.

Ava Shepherd (7)
Hindhayes Infant School, Street

Wish Me Luck Riddle

I have five pointy corners.
I have gold dust behind me.
I only come out at night.
I like shooting down in the night-time.
I see cars around me.
Everyone parks up to see me coming
through the sky.
What am I?

Answer: A shooting star.

Nikita Honey Manning-Bartlett (7)
Hindhayes Infant School, Street

Fun With Me

I have keys but no lock.
You can play with me loudly or sometimes quietly.
My keys are black and white.
I can have lessons with you.
You can have a lot of fun with me!
You can play tunes with me.
What am I?

Answer: A keyboard.

Ivy Davis (6)
Hindhayes Infant School, Street

Guess The Shape

I am a 2D shape.
I have four corners.
I have four sides.
My sides are all the same length.
You might see me in every country.
I am in your house everywhere.
You look through me every day.
What am I?

Answer: A square.

George Ware (6)
Hindhayes Infant School, Street

Rosie's Riddle

I sound like a duck but I'm not a duck.
I have a very long nose.
I have a very long tail.
I live in a hot desert.
I have a lovely, brown body.
I am very rough.
What am I?

Answer: A duck-billed platypus.

Rosie Payne (7)

Hindhayes Infant School, Street

Coby's Master Blaster

I am green.
I am spiky but sometimes I look fluffy.
You find me in deserts.
I can live outside and inside.
I am a plant but I don't need water.
I can sometimes hurt people.
What am I?

Answer: A cactus.

Coby Patey (7)
Hindhayes Infant School, Street

Meet The King

I look like a furry cat.
I sound like a screaming monkey.
I can be found in Longleat.
I have sharp teeth and sharp claws.
I am very, very noisy.
I feel soft and my fur is furry.
What am I?

Answer: A lion.

Alannah Pope (7)

Hindhayes Infant School, Street

Clever Cat

I am from the fearsome cat family.
I've got blazing speed.
When you see me, I am hunting for food.
I am a mammal.
I am famous for my speed.
My spots are black and brown.
What am I?

Answer: A cheetah.

Tegan London (7)
Hindhayes Infant School, Street

Dark Like The Night

It comes out at night.
It sleeps when it's day.
It starts with the letter 'B'.
It lives in a cave.
There are sometimes glow-worms above it.
It flaps like a bird.
What is it?

Answer: A bat.

Albie Walby (7)
Hindhayes Infant School, Street

Zane's Riddle

I am speedy but I'm fast too.
I have a turbo engine.
I race against people.
I jump ramps on the track.
I am number twenty-five on the track.
I win all the time.
What am I?

Answer: A racing car.

Zane James Hall (7)
Hindhayes Infant School, Street

Outrageous Bird

I have over eighty feathers.
I have three toes.
I go up to 462mph.
I have no teeth but I have a beak instead of teeth.
I don't have a nose.
I am deadly.
What am I?

Answer: A peregrine falcon.

Aiden Henry Curry (7)
Hindhayes Infant School, Street

Fun In The Garden

I look like a thing that people play on.
I sound squeaky.
You will find me in the garden.
I have long legs.
I feel hard and strange.
I am good to play with.
What am I?

Answer: Playing equipment.

Diasie Harmon (6)
Hindhayes Infant School, Street

What Am I?

I have four corners.
I have four sides.
You might see me as a window.
You might see me as a book.
You might see me as a table.
You might see me as a piece of paper.
What am I?

Answer: A square.

Benjamin Reaney (5)
Hindhayes Infant School, Street

Tiny And Shiny

He is spotty and likes leaves.
He goes in his shell in the day.
He is cute and shiny.
He is slow and steady.
He is beautiful in his heart.
He is shiny with love.
What is he?

Answer: A snail.

Freya Pate (7)
Hindhayes Infant School, Street

What Am I?

I have four sides.
You might see me as a blanket.
You see me as a piece of paper.
I have four corners.
You might see me as a window.
You might see me as a gate.
What am I?

Answer: A square.

Emily Carombayenin (6)
Hindhayes Infant School, Street

What Am I?

I have six faces.
Two of my faces are squares.
Four of my faces are rectangle.
I am a 3D shape.
I am the shape of a Spyker.
I am the shape of a building block.
What am I?

Answer: A cuboid.

Felicity Mobbs (6)
Hindhayes Infant School, Street

What Am I?

I have three pointy corners.
I have three sides.
My sides can be long or short.
I might be a sandwich.
You might cut me out.
You might see me on a road sign.
What am I?

Answer: A triangle.

Lily Holloway (6)
Hindhayes Infant School, Street

Osker's Riddle

I am from Mexico.
I have a crispy outside but a cheesy inside.
I have lettuce and tomato in me.
I feel very light and delicate.
You can eat me with your hands.
What am I?

Answer: A burrito.

Osker Guy-Gibbens (7)
Hindhayes Infant School, Street

Guess The Shape

I have four corners.
Two of my sides are longer than the others.
Two of my sides are shorter than the others.
I am a 2D shape.
I am the same shape as a door.
What am I?

Answer: A rectangle.

Henry Seaward (6)
Hindhayes Infant School, Street

The Best Teacher Ever!

She always wears high heels.
She is married.
She is a teacher.
She wears glasses.
Most of the time, she wears dresses.
She likes to have her nails done.
Who is she?

Answer: Mrs Flint.

Lydia Ferreira (7)
Hindhayes Infant School, Street

Juicy Grapes

I have a big stalk but I also have big pips.
I come in lots of different sizes.
I crunch when you bite me.
I can be made into juice.
I am usually red or green.
What am I?

Answer: An apple.

Eben Keith Pople (7)
Hindhayes Infant School, Street

Hello, Goodbye

I have three points and I'm short.
I have three corners, one is short, two are long.
I am a 2D shape.
I have no round edges.
I can stand up without legs.
What am I?

Answer: A triangle.

Estrid Durston (6)
Hindhayes Infant School, Street

Little Riddle

I am a 2D shape.
I am good for a digger's wheels.
I have no points.
I can roll on the floor like a ball.
You don't know if I'm the right way round.
What am I?

Answer: A circle.

Edith Whatley (5)
Hindhayes Infant School, Street

A Vegetable Riddle

I'm a vegetable.
I grow in the ground.
You can cook me.
Eat me and put me in a salad.
You can put me in a roast dinner.
I'm orange and crunchy.
What am I?

Answer: A carrot.

Daisy-Mae Rayner (7)
Hindhayes Infant School, Street

No More Tears Left To Cry!

She is a singer.
She is famous.
She has her nails done.
She has lots of hair.
She is in 'Sam & Cat'.
She is in 'Victorious'.
Who is she?

Answer: Ariana Grande.

Lacey Mai Fraser (8)
Hindhayes Infant School, Street

Guess My Answer

I have a circular face.
I have one point.
You might see me as a block.
You might see me after your ice cream.
I am on a bouncy castle.
I am a 3D shape.
What am I?

Answer: A cone.

Koby John Davey (6)
Hindhayes Infant School, Street

What Am I?

I have six faces.
You might see me like a piece of chocolate.
I am a 3D shape.
I look like a dice.
I am a box.
I look like a square but I am a window.
What am I?

Answer: A cube.

Faith Lenton (6)
Hindhayes Infant School, Street

Sharp Dagger

I have beady eyes.
I have sharp teeth.
I have four legs but they are not hands.
I have green all around me.
I have spikes on me.
I live in water.
What am I?

Answer: A crocodile.

Rex Bickham (7)
Hindhayes Infant School, Street

Little Red Riddle

They can be red and green.
They have leaves on them.
They are delicious.
They are something that you eat.
They are juicy and as red as a strawberry.
What are they?

Answer: Apples.

Tyler Jenson Foster (7)
Hindhayes Infant School, Street

Logan's Riddle

I feel furry.
I am found in Kashyyyk in Star Wars.
I sound like a bear growling but I have no ears.
I look like a bear.
I have brown and blonde fur.
What am I?

Answer: A Wookiee.

Logan Foster (7)

Hindhayes Infant School, Street

Absolutely Ridiculous Riddle!

I have two sides that are the same length.
You walk through me every day.
You may see me in the shape of a sign.
You may see me in the shape of paper.
What am I?

Answer: A rectangle.

Ava May Warren (6)
Hindhayes Infant School, Street

Guess The Shape

I look like a window.
I look like a card.
I look like a box.
I am a 2D shape.
I have four corners.
I have four sides that are the same length.
What am I?

Answer: A square.

Oscar Ware (6)
Hindhayes Infant School, Street

Brickster!

I am good for living in
I can be tall like a giraffe
I am made from bricks
I am from a city or town
I am hard to break
I have windows and doors
What am I?

Answer: A house.

Efe Selim (7)
Hindhayes Infant School, Street

What Am I?

I have four corners.
I have four sides the same length.
I have a 2D shape.
I won't be good for a cartwheel.
I could be a signpost for the road.
What am I?

Answer: A square.

Riley William Nicholls (6)
Hindhayes Infant School, Street

Jack's Riddle

I have sharp teeth and I am the king of all animals.
I have hairs on my face and I have hairs on my tail.
You will find me in the rocks and I have sharp claws.
What am I?

Answer: A lion.

Jack Robert Davis (7)
Hindhayes Infant School, Street

Guess What I Am

You might see me as a goal.
You might see me as a door.
You might see me as a table.
You might see me as a window.
You might see me as a board.
What am I?

Answer: A rectangle.

Mia Lee (5)

Hindhayes Infant School, Street

What Am I?

I can be on a sign next to the road.
I am a 2D shape.
I can be the teeth on a saw.
I have three sides and three corners.
I can be in your lunch.
What am I?

Answer: A triangle.

Abe Evans (6)
Hindhayes Infant School, Street

Little Riddle

It has long ears.
It has two pointy teeth.
It has four legs.
It has a fluffy tail.
You can see it in a zoo.
Its nose twitches all the time.
What is it?

Answer: A rabbit.

Lilly Christine Harrison (6)
Hindhayes Infant School, Street

Little Riddle

It is grey.
It has a long trunk.
It is scared of lions.
It has spots.
It likes to suck and gulp food.
It likes to play in the dirt.
What is it?

Answer: An anteater.

Kieran Wigley (7)
Hindhayes Infant School, Street

My Riddle

I sometimes have holes in me.
I am yellow but sometimes I have red skin.
Mice like to eat me.
I make you feel happy inside.
I am good to eat.
What am I?

Answer: Cheese.

Ellie Joy Sparks (7)
Hindhayes Infant School, Street

What Am I?

I have four corners.
I have four straight sides.
My sides are all the same.
You might see me in a house.
You might see me as a sandwich.
What am I?

Answer: A square.

Jessica Daisy Jordan (6)
Hindhayes Infant School, Street

Shape Sizzler

I have a wrapper around me.
I have no sides.
I have five corners.
I have two triangles.
I have six straight sides.
I live in a box.
What am I?

Answer: A sweet.

Lily-Mae Creed (7)
Hindhayes Infant School, Street

Nutty Riddle

I sound like an engine.
You find me in the town.
I have four wheels.
I am in different colours.
I have a boot but I cannot pull a trailer.
What am I?

Answer: A car.

Oscar Frank Nutt (7)
Hindhayes Infant School, Street

In The Sky

I am really white.
I can be really dark.
I am friends with the sun.
I am fluffy.
I am made out of water.
I look like candyfloss.
What am I?

Answer: A cloud.

Tyler Hiscox (7)

Hindhayes Infant School, Street

Guess The Shape

I have a point.
My faces are triangles.
I am 3D.
You can see me in the desert.
I can get mummies out of me and I have skulls in me.
What am I?

Answer: A pyramid.

Finlay Duncan Lamb (6)
Hindhayes Infant School, Street

What Am I?

I have six sides.
I have six corners.
I have one face.
I am not curved.
I might be the shape of a honeycomb.
I am a 2D shape.
What am I?

Answer: A hexagon.

Ben Rios Smith (6)

Hindhayes Infant School, Street

Meet The Silly Girl

I have pointy ears.
I have a long tail.
I have sharp teeth.
I have ginger skin but I have black and white spots.
I feel like sleeping.
What am I?

Answer: A cat.

Sophie Winter (7)
Hindhayes Infant School, Street

A Fluffy Delight

I make no noise.
You find me in a pet shop.
I have long ears.
I am cute but I can scratch.
I look like a marble.
I feel soft.
What am I?

Answer: A rabbit.

Lois Durston (7)
Hindhayes Infant School, Street

My Riddle

I live in the jungle.
I am the king of the jungle.
My name starts with 'L'.
I am fluffy.
I eat meat.
I have four feet.
What am I?

Answer: A lion.

Josh Francis (6)
Hindhayes Infant School, Street

What Is It?

It is a sport.
You can get injured.
It is very long.
Ten people on each side.
You can kick one thing.
You can lose or win.
What is it?

Answer: Football.

Alfie Turner (7)
Hindhayes Infant School, Street

Sharp Teeth

I have four legs.
I have some long fur.
I have sticky-up ears.
I have a long tail.
I have long legs.
I have a big face.
What am I?

Answer: A cat.

Darcy Jeffery (7)
Hindhayes Infant School, Street

Cute Pet

I have a fluffy tail.
I go *miaow!*
I have straight ears.
I am cute and soft.
I am fast at running.
I am small.
What am I?

Answer: A cat.

Reegan Ollie John Smith (7)
Hindhayes Infant School, Street

The Silliest Riddle Ever

I am a 2D shape.
I have four corners.
I have four sides.
I look like a slice of bread.
My sides are the same length.
What am I?

Answer: A square.

Daisy Russell (6)
Hindhayes Infant School, Street

Lauren's Riddle

I have a long tongue.
You will find me in the jungle.
I don't make a sound.
I look like I'm slimy but I am dry.
What am I?

Answer: A snake.

Lauren Parsons (7)
Hindhayes Infant School, Street

Big Animal

It has dots on it.
It is red.
In the summer, it comes out.
It normally lives on leaves.
It lives in gardens.
What is it?

Answer: A ladybird.

Ava-Grace Payne (7)
Hindhayes Infant School, Street

Zoom! Zoom!

I am a predator
I am a meat eater
I may eat you
I am spotty
I am yellow
I am the fastest animal on land
What am I?

Answer: A cheetah.

Jacob Wood (7)
Hindhayes Infant School, Street

What Am I?

I can be the teeth on a saw.
I am a 2D shape.
I can be an arrow.
I can be on a sign.
I have three corners.
What am I?

Answer: A triangle.

Barnaby Richards (6)
Hindhayes Infant School, Street

Ridiculous Riddle

I am a 2D shape.
I have four sides.
Two of my sides are longer than the others.
You walk through me every day.
What am I?

Answer: A rectangle.

Ollie Hall (6)

Hindhayes Infant School, Street

Banana Alien

I like to eat meat.
I feel fluffy.
I am bigger than a cheetah.
I feel soft.
I am fast.
I am very long.
What am I?

Answer: A tiger.

Christian Dumitru (7)
Hindhayes Infant School, Street

Guess The Shape

I have six corners.
I have six sides.
I have sharp corners.
I do not have three corners.
I am a 2D shape.
What am I?

Answer: A hexagon.

Olivia Solomons (6)
Hindhayes Infant School, Street

Hot Wheels

I have a seat.
I move gently and fast.
I have really big bars.
I have two wheels that wiggle.
I have a bell.
What am I?

Answer: A bike.

Conner Collard (7)
Hindhayes Infant School, Street

Everyone's Favourite Treat

It is brown.
It is yummy.
It is a square.
It gets wrapped in a cover.
You can buy it in a shop.
What is it?

Answer: A chocolate bar.

Lilly Thompson (7)
Hindhayes Infant School, Street

Guess The Shape

I have one face.
I am round.
I am curved.
I am flat.
I am a 2D shape.
I am shaped like a plate.
What am I?

Answer: A circle.

Zackery Austwick (6)
Hindhayes Infant School, Street

Guess My Shape

You might see me fly.
I have four corners.
I have four sides.
I am a 2D shape.
I have sticks in me.
What am I?

Answer: A kite.

Aaron Browne (6)
Hindhayes Infant School, Street

2D Shape

I have curved sides.
I have four sides.
I have three ends.
I have two short sides and two long sides.
What am I?

Answer: A circle.

Oliver Larkman (5)
Hindhayes Infant School, Street

Little Riddle

I have three points.
I have three straight sides.
I am a 2D shape.
I can be a slice of watermelon.
What am I?

Answer: A triangle.

Betsy Anne Harrison (6)
Hindhayes Infant School, Street

Guess The Shape

I have three corners.
You can see me as a flag.
You can see me as a roof.
I have three sides.
What am I?

Answer: A triangle.

Joshua Joseph Bryan (6)
Hindhayes Infant School, Street

Little Riddle

I have four corners.
I have four sides.
My sides are the same length.
I am good for a patio.
What am I?

Answer: A square.

Daisy Alice Spencer (5)
Hindhayes Infant School, Street

What Am I?

I am the same shape as a door.
I am a 2D shape.
I have four corners.
I have four sides.
What am I?

Answer: A rectangle.

Archie Pickles (6)
Hindhayes Infant School, Street

What Am I?

I am a flat shape.
I have four corners.
I have four sides.
I am the shape of a window.
What am I?

Answer: A square.

Callum York Rivers (6), Kaydn, Lola, Lily Spurrell, Zack & Grace Mathias-Lukins (6)
Hindhayes Infant School, Street

What Am I?

I am a 2D shape.
You might see me in a beehive.
I have six sides.
I have six points.
What am I?

Answer: A hexagon.

Betsy Alice Beatrice Gamble (6)
Hindhayes Infant School, Street

Little Riddle

I have four sides.
I have four corners.
Two sides are longer.
I am a 2D shape.
What am I?

Answer: A rectangle.

Jacob Hunter (6)
Hindhayes Infant School, Street

The Lost Shape

I have four sides.
I look like a custard cream.
I look like the back of a truck.
What am I?

Answer: A rectangle.

Rohan Slaughter-Ware (6)
Hindhayes Infant School, Street

Guess The Shape

I have four corners.
I have four sides.
I can be a window.
I can be a book.
What am I?

Answer: A square.

Francesco Cinque (6)
Hindhayes Infant School, Street

Guess The 3D Shape

It has three faces
It can be used for a glue stick
It looks like a circle
What is it?

Answer: A cylinder.

Ada Hole (6)
Hindhayes Infant School, Street

2D Shape

I could be used as a slide.
There are three sides.
I am long and pointy.
What am I?

Answer: A triangle.

Ava-Grace Carter (5)
Hindhayes Infant School, Street

I Am A 3D Shape

I have six faces.
I can be used as an ice cube.
I have eight pointy edges.
What am I?

Answer: A cube.

Poppy Thompson (5)
Hindhayes Infant School, Street

A Sticky Mess

I am yummy.
I am round.
I have syrup on me.
I am cooked in a pan.
What am I?

Answer: A pancake.

Alanna Reed (7)

Hindhayes Infant School, Street

What Am I?

I have four corners.
I have four sides.
You might see me as a sandwich.
What am I?

Answer: A square.

Ava Spencer (6)
Hindhayes Infant School, Street

What Am I?

I have three corners.
I have three sides.
I have one straight line.
What am I?

Answer: A triangle.

Maisy Pickersgill (6)
Hindhayes Infant School, Street

What Am I?

I have four sides.
I look like a football pitch.
I look like an iPad.
What am I?

Answer: A square.

Noémie Berry (6)
Hindhayes Infant School, Street

The Amazing Shape

I have four sides.
I have four points.
My sides are the same length.
What am I?

Answer: A square.

Mia Susan Whitty (6)
Hindhayes Infant School, Street

2D Shape

I have a curved face
I have no points
I have no straight sides
What am I?

Answer: A circle.

Freddie Cooper (6)
Hindhayes Infant School, Street

Guess The Shape

I am a 3D shape.
I have no corners.
I am a good football.
What am I?

Answer: A sphere.

Oscar Budden (6)
Hindhayes Infant School, Street

Guess My Shape

My shape is round
I have one round face
I have no points
What am I?

Answer: A sphere.

Joseph Dolman (6)
Hindhayes Infant School, Street

What Am I?

I have a curved face
I am round
I am used as a ball
What am I?

Answer: A semicircle.

Ella-Grace Tully (6)
Hindhayes Infant School, Street

I Am 3D

You can use me as a cube.
I have sides.
I have a face.
What am I?

Answer: A square.

Archie Wall (6)
Hindhayes Infant School, Street

Sun

I have no points.
I have a face.
I look like the sun.
What am I?

Answer: A circle.

Elif Selim (6)

Hindhayes Infant School, Street

Round

I am round.
I have no points.
I have one curved edge.
What am I?

Answer: A circle.

Florence Elsie Jane Turner (6)
Hindhayes Infant School, Street

What Am I?

I am round.
I am fat.
You can use me as a football.
What am I?

Answer: A sphere.

Bliss Ann-Harwood Moulder (6)
Hindhayes Infant School, Street

The Beauty Of Me

It's so strong it does not break.
It's so powerful it penetrates a lake.
Sometimes it's as weak as a twig left in the sun.
It's so wonderful, it gives us the power to have fun.
Without it, we could not see the difference between you and me.
You can get it from the sun but it's also man-made.
What is it?

Answer: Light.

Archie Devlin (6)
Manorside Combined School, Parkstone

What Am I?

I live in the forest.
I swing from tree to tree.
I hang from my hands and feet, always looking for treats to eat.
Bananas are my favourite thing to eat.
Bananas grow nearby, which soon catch my eye!
My tail swings side to side as I feel happy that I have my meal.
What am I?

Answer: A monkey.

Lacey-Mae Bond (5)

Manorside Combined School, Parkstone

Under The Sea

I have lots of arms but no fingers.
I have no legs but I can swim backwards.
I use ink but not to write.
I have a beak but I am not a bird.
I have a big head but I am not an alien.
I have three hearts, nine brains and blue blood.
What am I?

Answer: An octopus.

Rachel Lewis (6)
Manorside Combined School, Parkstone

Roar

I live in the jungle and chase my food.
My fur is orange with black stripes.
My claws are as sharp as a kitchen knife.
I scare other animals away with my noisy roar.
When I am hunting, I swish my long tail from side to side.
What am I?

Answer: A tiger.

Mitchell Sailer (6)

Manorside Combined School, Parkstone

My Holiday

I am golden in colour.
I am something that's so small.
I am made into a castle, although I'm not a brick.
I might get into your food.
I can be held in the palm of your hand.
I am something you find on a beach.
What am I?

Answer: Sand.

Paige Louise Jackson (6)
Manorside Combined School, Parkstone

Only Time Will Tell

I have a face without eyes.
I have two hands but no fingers.
I have no mouth but I make a continuous sound.
I don't walk but I move around.
Sometimes I go backwards or forwards.
I never stop moving.
What am I?

Answer: A clock.

Danny Williamson-Jeff (6)
Manorside Combined School, Parkstone

Tiny Friend

I am very small.
I have tiny legs.
I can have different colours.
I love to eat leaves.
My friends are beetles, snails, grasshoppers and spiders.
When I grow big, I become a butterfly.
What am I?

Answer: A caterpillar.

Sara Mazhar (5)
Manorside Combined School, Parkstone

Precious

I cry a lot but I don't talk.
I like to sleep a lot but not during the night.
I have tiny hands and feet but I have no teeth.
I look around a lot but I don't walk.
What am I?

Answer: A newborn baby.

Alicia Dalewska (6)
Manorside Combined School, Parkstone

To Grow

I start as small as a seed.
I have no feet but I move in the wind.
I need sunshine to live.
If I get picked, I will die.
I live with worms.
I need water to grow.
What am I?

Answer: A plant.

Rowan Penzer (5)
Manorside Combined School, Parkstone

Furry Friends

Hay is my favourite.
I like to hop and play.
People like to stroke me.
I love to sleep in hay.
I sometimes live underground.
In a field, I can also be found.
What am I?

Answer: A rabbit.

Alana Nicole Mattock (6)
Manorside Combined School, Parkstone

Extinct

I am a dinosaur.
I only eat meat.
I have a sail on my back.
I walk on two legs.
I have been found in North Africa.
I lived in the Cretaceous period.
What am I?

Answer: A spinosaurus.

Jake Bradford (6)
Manorside Combined School, Parkstone

Holiday Destination

I am in France.
You can go on rides.
You can meet characters.
You can get autographs.
Everyone enjoys being here.
America has one too.
What am I?

Answer: Disneyland.

Lorelei Render (5)
Manorside Combined School, Parkstone

Magical Colours

I have seven colours.
Everybody is happy when they see me.
I am sparkly and high in the sky.
I come after rain.
My shape is an arch.
What am I?

Answer: A rainbow.

Cathaleya Titeica (6)
Manorside Combined School, Parkstone

Precious Place

I have a roof.
I am made of bricks.
I have windows.
I have people inside.
Cashiers work in me.
People keep their money in me.
What am I?

Answer: A bank.

Tola Slezak (6)
Manorside Combined School, Parkstone

A Type Of Crossing

I am white and black
I like to eat plants
I live in Africa
I have four hooves
I have a mane
I have a long tail
What am I?

Answer: A zebra.

Luca Luigi Raccagni (6)
Manorside Combined School, Parkstone

Fantasy Animal

I have a beautiful tail.
I live in a magical forest.
I can fly.
I am pink and white.
I look like a horse.
What am I?

Answer: A unicorn.

Mia Jones (6)
Manorside Combined School, Parkstone

My Friend At Home

I purr.
I have short ears.
I do not go for walks.
I talk a lot.
I have sharp claws.
I have a long tail.
What am I?

Answer: A cat.

Macy Holder (5)
Manorside Combined School, Parkstone

Cunning Carnivore

I am extinct.
I am tiny.
I am a carnivore.
I am dangerous.
I have sharp claws.
I hunt for my prey.
What am I?

Answer: A raptor.

Isaac Patterson (6)
Manorside Combined School, Parkstone

What Am I?

I am yellow
I am spotty
I am orange
I have four legs
I have a big face
What am I?

Answer: A giraffe.

Sophia Marie Ekomwenrenren (6)
Manorside Combined School, Parkstone

Delicate

I am colourful and delicate.
I have six tiny legs.
I have long antennae that help me look for flowers.
I used to be a caterpillar.
I can be lots of beautiful colours and patterns.
I taste horrible because I eat milkweed leaves!
What am I?

Answer: A butterfly.

Liliana Sala (6)
St Walburga's Catholic Primary School, Moordown

Busy Worker

I have six legs.
I can fly and I have two antennae.
I have five eyes.
I have one sting.
I have three body parts and I have furry legs.
I have four wings and I have one tongue.
I have black legs and I have stripes.
What am I?

Answer: A bee.

Adorn Thottuvayayil (6)
St Walburga's Catholic Primary School, Moordown

Very Delicate

I can fly.
I have black legs.
I have black markings on my head.
I can fly quite fast.
I have six black spots on my back.
I have four wings.
I have five eyes.
I have white markings on my head.
What am I?

Answer: A ladybird.

Toby Garcia (6)
St Walburga's Catholic Primary School, Moordown

Busy Workers

I work for a queen.
I have five eyes.
I suck nectar from the flowers.
I have black legs.
I have one tongue.
I have two antennae.
I have one sting.
I have three body parts.
I have six legs.
What am I?

Answer: A bee.

Lilly Reynolds (6)

St Walburga's Catholic Primary School, Moordown

Bouncy

I am bouncy like a kangaroo.
I am camouflaged to look like a leaf.
I have six long legs.
I like long, wavy grass.
I have four delicate wings.
I think grass and leaves are delicate.
What am I?

Answer: A grasshopper.

Alfie Cooper (6)
St Walburga's Catholic Primary School, Moordown

Green And Bouncy!

Sometimes I am camouflaged.
I jump like a kangaroo.
I am the colour of a spring leaf.
I like long, wavy grass.
I have four delicate wings.
I need to stay away from frogs and newts!
What am I?

Answer: A grasshopper.

Bobby McGowan (6)
St Walburga's Catholic Primary School, Moordown

Beautiful

I have colourful, beautiful wings.
I have patterns on my wings.
I am delicate.
I like bright flowers.
I used to be a caterpillar.
I am a very beautiful insect.
What am I?

Answer: A butterfly.

Imogen Rose Smith (6)
St Walburga's Catholic Primary School, Moordown

Green And Jumpy!

I can jump very high.
My tongue is very long.
I eat delicious flies.
I live in a cool pond.
I start my life as a wriggly tadpole.
My throat blows up like a ball.
What am I?

Answer: A frog.

Chris Antwi (6)

St Walburga's Catholic Primary School, Moordown

Jumpy

I have spots on my skin.
I am bigger than an insect.
I can have lumps on my back.
My eyes bulge out of my head.
My feet are webbed.
I do not have any antennae.
What am I?

Answer: A frog.

Joshua Matthews (6)
St Walburga's Catholic Primary School, Moordown

Chasey

I have four hundred legs.
I like fresh green leaves.
I have two antennae.
I have nineteen body parts.
I lay lots of eggs.
I can coil into a spiral.
What am I?

Answer: A millipede.

Harry Samuel Jose (6)
St Walburga's Catholic Primary School, Moordown

Crawling

I have a hard shell.
I have six legs.
I can run really fast.
It is very difficult to catch me.
I am an insect.
I have a shiny, green shell.
What am I?

Answer: A beetle.

Catalina Mya Arbelaez Correa (6)
St Walburga's Catholic Primary School, Moordown

Spotty

I have antennae.
I come from a pupa.
I have two soft wings and two hard wings.
I have six legs.
I eat other insects.
I live in a garden.
What am I?

Answer: A ladybird.

Freya Murray (6)
St Walburga's Catholic Primary School, Moordown

Dance Flash

I am colourful.
I have four wings.
I live near ponds.
I can fly.
I live in a nest.
I am shiny.
I can fly super fast in a flash.
What am I?

Answer: A dragonfly.

Ellie Grace Samath Nicholson (6)
St Walburga's Catholic Primary School, Moordown

Pest Muncher

I have six legs.
I can fly.
I eat juicy leaves.
I have some spots.
I have white markings.
I have two hard wings and two soft wings.
What am I?

Answer: A ladybird.

Cianán McCaffrey (5)
St Walburga's Catholic Primary School, Moordown

Change

I have lots of legs.
I like leaves.
I have lots of body parts.
When I grow up, I will fly.
I eat vegetables.
I have strong jaws.
What am I?

Answer: A caterpillar.

Katie Fendley (6)
St Walburga's Catholic Primary School, Moordown

Hairy

I have eight legs.
I can live outside and inside.
I am hairy.
I make beautiful webs.
I eat flies.
I can't stick to my own web.
What am I?

Answer: A spider.

Lulu Jenkins (5)
St Walburga's Catholic Primary School, Moordown

Hard Workers

I have six legs.
I can flutter from flower to flower.
I have four delicate wings.
I am colourful.
I am delicate.
I am a minibeast.
What am I?

Answer: A bee.

Maria Pickering (6)
St Walburga's Catholic Primary School, Moordown

Small And Smart!

I am little.
I am very strong.
I eat leaves.
I am black.
I make and live on a special hill.
I don't have wings.
What am I?

Answer: An ant.

Ellie Parry (6)

St Walburga's Catholic Primary School, Moordown

Roller

I curl up into a ball
I live under logs
I have white babies
I have fourteen legs
I am dark brown
I have armour
What am I?

Answer: A woodlouse.

Adam Bujak (6)
St Walburga's Catholic Primary School, Moordown

Fast Flyer

I live in a garden.
I have six legs.
I fly with four wings.
I eat aphids.
I have two soft wings and two hard wings.
What am I?

Answer: A ladybird.

Eden Grant (6)
St Walburga's Catholic Primary School, Moordown

I Am A Fast Walker

I have lots of legs.
I eat leaves.
I can walk fast.
I am black and shiny.
I am long.
I can roll into a coil.
What am I?

Answer: A millipede.

Oliver Lloyd (6)
St Walburga's Catholic Primary School, Moordown

Creepy

I have furry legs.
I like wrapping flies up.
I can bite you.
I am not an insect.
I am dangerous.
I am scary.
What am I?

Answer: A spider.

Stanley Bagnall (6)
St Walburga's Catholic Primary School, Moordown

Crawler

I have fourteen legs.
I have a smooth, hard back.
I hide under shady logs.
I live outside.
I am not an insect.
What am I?

Answer: A woodlouse.

Erin Barber-Miller (6)
St Walburga's Catholic Primary School, Moordown

Colourful

I have two wings.
I am delicate.
I am colourful.
I can fly.
I like plants and flowers.
I have a pattern.
What am I?

Answer: A butterfly.

Jaden Legaspi-Harvey (6)
St Walburga's Catholic Primary School, Moordown

Buzz

I have wings.
I have three body parts.
I have one stinger.
I have six legs.
I have stripes.
I collect nectar.
What am I?

Answer: A bee.

Autumn Hume (6)
St Walburga's Catholic Primary School, Moordown

I Like The River

I am shiny.
I can fly quickly.
I am an insect and I am colourful.
I have big eyes.
I live near the water.
What am I?

Answer: A dragonfly.

Sofia Jakubowska (6)
St Walburga's Catholic Primary School, Moordown

Big

I have eight legs.
I eat yucky things!
I lay eggs.
I have eight long legs.
I am hairy.
I sit on a web.
What am I?

Answer: A spider.

Noah Abonyi (6)
St Walburga's Catholic Primary School, Moordown

Buzz

I make honey.
I am stripy.
I am yellow and black.
I collect nectar.
I am small.
I work hard for my queen!
What am I?

Answer: A bee.

Freya Comman (5)
St Walburga's Catholic Primary School, Moordown

Spots

I have spots.
I lay yellow eggs.
I can fly.
I am usually red and black.
I am small.
I am an insect.
What am I?

Answer: A ladybird.

Maja Boroszko (6)
St Walburga's Catholic Primary School, Moordown

Spotty

I have black spots
I have wings
I have legs
I like to fly
I am usually red and black
I live outside
What am I?

Answer: A ladybird.

Zofia Tomczyk (6)
St Walburga's Catholic Primary School, Moordown

Super Speedy

I have furry legs.
I carry bags of pollen.
I can fly.
My wings are delicate.
I am small.
I am stripy.
What am I?

Answer: A bee.

Violet Wasmuth (6)
St Walburga's Catholic Primary School, Moordown

Scary!

I have long wings.
I eat yucky food.
I am brown.
I can fly.
I have six legs.
I have antennae.
What am I?

Answer: A cockroach.

Juliette Pegrum (6)
St Walburga's Catholic Primary School, Moordown

Speedy Flyer

I have six furry legs
I have a sting
I have a big, furry body
I am black and yellow
I collect pollen
What am I?

Answer: A bee.

Dixie Garton (5)

St Walburga's Catholic Primary School, Moordown

Spotty

I am small
I have six legs
I have wings
I have antennae
I have lots of spots
I can fly
What am I?

Answer: A ladybird.

Elizabeth Stalley (6)
St Walburga's Catholic Primary School, Moordown

Buzz

I am an insect.
I am stripy.
I am hairy.
I make honey.
I am small.
What am I?

Answer: A bee.

Sunday Assey (5)
St Walburga's Catholic Primary School, Moordown

Sting

I am delicate
I am colourful
I can sting
I can fly
What am I?

Answer: A bee.

Ziyana-Jean Clark (6)
St Walburga's Catholic Primary School, Moordown

Sneaky

I'm camouflaged
I'm wrinkly
I'm scaly
I'm cautious
I pretend I'm not there
I like sunbathing
I like eating leaves
I can change colour
What am I?

Answer: A chameleon.

Kitty Taschner (7)
Sunninghill Preparatory School, South Walks

Down From The Sky

I come down from the sky.
Down like lightning, I float.
I am so beautiful, people love me.
You don't see me too often.
I am cool and soft.
I am unique.
What am I?

Answer: A snowflake.

Iris Høyvåg (6)
Sunninghill Preparatory School, South Walks

Home Sweet Home

I am not alive
I am made of natural materials
I am a home
I am brown
I am built by a creature that has no arms
and loves worms!
I am a safe place
What am I?

Answer: A nest.

William Hall (7)
Sunninghill Preparatory School, South Walks

Dinosaurs

I lived 250 million years ago
I eat fish
I am extinct
I have one paddle
I have sharp teeth
I am like a dolphin
What am I?

Answer: An ichthyosaurs.

Gregory A Vaisyan (7)
Sunninghill Preparatory School, South Walks

Watch Out!

I am not furry
I am a plant eater
I have four legs
I live on land
I am black and white
You can't cuddle me
What am I?

Answer: A porcupine.

Charlie Flower (7)
Sunninghill Preparatory School, South Walks

What Am I?

I have red eyes.
I have three legs on each side.
I have little wings.
I can fly.
I am black.
I am quite small.
What am I?

Answer: A fly.

Anna Wright (6)
Sunninghill Preparatory School, South Walks

On And On

I am as long as when time began
I am forever
I go on and on
I am a war
I am a family
I change every minute
What am I?

Answer: History.

Samuel Laurence Roger Lawn (7)
Sunninghill Preparatory School, South Walks

Lightning

I am spotty.
I am black, yellow and furry.
I am fast.
I don't play fair!
I eat meat.
I am a mammal.
What am I?

Answer: A cheetah.

Clara Telfer (7)
Sunninghill Preparatory School, South Walks

What Am I?

I live in the woods
I am scaly
I have a long tongue
I eat bugs
I am green (sometimes)
I have four legs
What am I?

Answer: A gecko.

Rex Woollam (7)
Sunninghill Preparatory School, South Walks

YoungWriters
Est.1991

YOUNG WRITERS INFORMATION

We hope you have enjoyed reading this book – and that you will continue to in the coming years.

If you're a young writer who enjoys reading and creative writing, or the parent of an enthusiastic poet or story writer, do visit our website **www.youngwriters.co.uk**. Here you will find free competitions, workshops and games, as well as recommended reads, a poetry glossary and our blog.

If you would like to order further copies of this book, or any of our other titles, then please give us a call or visit **www.youngwriters.co.uk**.

Young Writers
Remus House
Coltsfoot Drive
Peterborough
PE2 9BF
(01733) 890066
info@youngwriters.co.uk